God's Unblinkable Eyes

Written by Jane Efua Asamoah

Illustrated by Patrick Noze

God's Unblinkable Eyes
Copyright © 2021 by Jane Efua Asamoah
All rights reserved.

Cover Image Source Credit: NASA, NOAO, ESA, the Hubble Helix Nebula Team, M. Meixner (STScI) and T.A. Rector (NRAO)

No part of this publication may be reproduced, stored in a retrieval system, or transmitted in any form or by any means—electronic, mechanical, photocopy, recording, or any other—without the prior permission of the author(s) or editor.

Paperback ISBN: 978-1-950685-75-2

Hardcover ISBN: 978-1-950685-79-0

To my husband, Owusu –
for your encouragement.

"The eyes of the LORD
are everywhere."
—Proverbs 15:3a

"Mom, can I have a staring contest with God like I do with my brother?" seven-year-old Kojo asks as he and his mom talk about the human eye.

Mom looks at Kojo, surprised by his question. "That sounds interesting, Buddy! You know God is a Spirit, right?" Kojo nods his head. "Since He is a Spirit, and you cannot see Him like you see your brother, how are you going to have a staring contest with Him?"

"Well, I can't see Him, but He can see me!" Kojo replies excitedly.

"You are absolutely right, Son. He can see you . . . He can even see inside of you," Mom replies with a laugh, softly tickling Kojo's tummy with her finger.

"How can God see inside of me? How's that possible, Mommy?" Kojo asks.

"Because He is the one who created all of you, including your inward parts. Did you know that God's eyes saw you even before you were born—while you were still in my tummy? He put together all the small, delicate parts that make up your body, like your fingers and toes and heart and lungs."

"God can see inside us?" Kojo questions, even more puzzled at the thought of God seeing Him in his mommy's tummy.

"Yes, God is able to see all that because He is OMNISCIENT!" Mom tells Kojo. "Can you say that with me?"

"Ahm-ni-shent." Kojo and Mom repeat the word together, then Mom says, "Omniscient means ALL KNOWING. That's how God knew you before you were born!" Kojo's eyes widen in wonder.

"On the day you were born," Mom continues, "God looked at you and said you looked really good because you look like Him. You are the apple of His eye."

"What does that mean, Mommy?" Kojo asks.

"That means you are very special to God and you are loved by Him," Mom answers.

"God's eyes see the end from the beginning. Every day of your life has already been recorded in His book—even the days that you haven't lived yet. God's eyes have already seen every single day, hour, minute, and second of your life. God's eyes have already seen your future, and He says it is incredibly good."

"God's eyes never leave you from the time you get up in the morning till the time you go to bed at night. God's eyes watch you all through each night while you sleep."

"Mom, doesn't God need to sleep?" Kojo asks.

"God's eyes do not ever close in sleep, and they never need to rest for a little bit to have the strength to watch over us. He never sleeps, and He does not take naps. In fact, there's no nighttime for sleeping where God lives," Mom tells Kojo.

"That's really amazing!" Kojo says. "Where does God live?" he asks.

"God lives in heaven with a host of angels. They are too many to count. Do you know that you have guardian angels?"

"Who are guardian angels?" Kojo asks.

"Guardian angels are like your personal security guards. God has commanded them to guide and protect you."

"Are my guardian angels with me when I'm waiting for the school bus?" Kojo asks.

"Yes, Son. They are with you everywhere you go. You cannot see them with your physical eye, but they can see you because God has assigned them to guard you."

Kojo is delighted at the thought of having guardian angels.

"Not only does God see your guardian angels but sees every strand of hair on your head and can even count them because He is . . ."

"OMNISCIENT!!" Kojo quickly finishes off Mom's sentence with a thundering reply. Kojo remembers how he loves to comb his hair when he's dressing himself for school.

"Mom, is God able to count all the different types of hair my classmates have? Kojo asks.

"Yes, because . . ."

"I know, I know! Because He's OMNISCIENT!!" Kojo interrupts with excitement.

"During the day, God's eyes continue to watch over you when you leave your house and when you come home. He sees you when you play with the neighborhood kids. God not only sees us here in our house, but He sees everyone in every house in our neighborhood."

"Kojo, I want you to think about all the different houses in our neighborhood, the families who live in each house, and each person in each family. God's eyes see every child and every adult in every family, everywhere in the whole world at the same time."

"Mom, do you mean God can see William right next door and Grandma in Ghana at the same time?" Kojo asks.

"Yes, He can because He is . . ."

"OMNISCIENT!!" Kojo proudly replies.

"God's eyes see everyone in every neighborhood in our city. He sees everything in every city in our state, every state in our country, and every country on our continent. In fact, God sees everything about everyone on all seven continents on our planet. God's eyes see everything, everywhere at the same time. He is OMNISCIENT!!"

"Mom, God sees the planets! That is so cool!" Kojo exclaims.

"Yes, Buddy! God sees all the planets. His eyes see the whole universe at the same time. He sees the moon, stars, and the sun. God's eyes see each and every star and know them all by name. Imagine everything in outer space that astronomers have not even discovered yet. God's eyes see all of that, too, because He created all of it," Mom answers.

"Son, there's so much more to know about God's eyes. God's eyes see every flower, tree, and plant that blossoms beautifully year after year in all places around the world."

"God's eyes can see each grain of sand and can even count them."

"God's eyes can even see every creature in the ocean, all the way down to the deepest places."

"M-o-m! Do God's eyes need fancy goggles to see everything under the sea?"

"No, Son. We do, but God doesn't. From the tiniest to the largest sea creature, God's eyes see all of them because He is . . ."

"OMNISCIENT!!" Kojo joyfully responds.

"God's eyes see every kind of animal here on earth. Think of all the animals you know."

"God's eyes do not miss any of the birds that fly in the sky."

"God's eyes capture what we cannot see with the naked eye. God's eyes see even the invisible organisms we can see only with a microscope."

"Mom, can God see what's in my heart?" Kojo asks.

"God's eyes see everything in our hearts and every thought in our minds. God's eyes see the secret things we are hiding there. God's eyes see good and bad. Remember, He is OMNISCIENT! God's eyes do not miss anything we are doing here on earth. He knows everything about you and me and yet still loves us. God's eyes are full of love, and He wants us to love each other. It makes Him sad when we don't listen to Him, just like it makes me sad when you don't listen to me and I'm forced to put you in time out."

"God's eyes are full of compassion. He longs for everyone to come to His Son Jesus for help."

"God's eyes see a whole bunch of things, and I'm sure there are a whole lot more I may not have even thought of to share with you."

"WOW! God's eyes are really incredible, Mom!" exclaims Kojo.

"Yes, they are! And the amazing part is, He sees EVERYTHING at the same time because HE IS OMNISCIENT!"

"I'd love for you to imagine God's eyes as never blinking—as Him never taking His eyes off of you, even for the fraction of a moment it would take to blink. I'm glad that even though God has to look at so many things all at once, each one of us is God's favorite. God watches over you, Kojo, as if you were the only one in the entire universe."

Mom gives Kojo a really big hug.

"I hope that one day when you see Him face-to-face, maybe you can ask Him to have a staring contest with you. Though I already know who will win, I'm sure it'll be a whole lot of fun."

About the Author

Jane E. Asamoah was born and raised in Ghana, West Africa. She lives in Roanoke, Virginia, with her husband and their three precious boys. She is the author of My Mommy's Name Is Mommy. She will be serving as the new children's supervisor for Bible Study Fellowship starting this fall. Her heart is to encourage parents to be intentional about helping their children understand God's Word. The Bible instructs parents not to keep God's Word to themselves but to tell it to their children so that they in turn will tell it to their own children and enable the next generation to know God (Ps. 78:1-8).

About the Illustrator

Patrick Noze was born in Haiti in the province of Jeremie 'City of Poets.' He is a third generation sculptor and painter. "I am always thinking about the wonders of the world from its simplest to its most complex shapes. To my eyes, the world is a large canvas. Everything I see, dream or I encounter I use as an inspiration for my work." He attended Pratt Institute, School of Art and Science. He is presently very involved in his community and serves on a voluntary basis on the Advisory Council for Art in Cultural Affairs. He lives in Orange County, Florida, with his family.

www.ingramcontent.com/pod-product-compliance
Lightning Source LLC
Chambersburg PA
CBHW051403110526
44592CB00023B/2933